W9-BAH-843

Moments for Fathers

by Robert Strand

First printing, February 1994
Seventh printing, January 2006

Copyright © 1993 by New Leaf Press. All rights reserved. No part of this book may be used or reproduced in any manner whatsoever without written permission of the publisher except in the case of brief quotations in articles and reviews. For information write: New Leaf Press, Inc., P.O. Box 726, Green Forest, AR 72638.

ISBN: 0-89221-263-2
Library of Congress Catalog Number: 93-87692

Cover design by Left Coast Design, Portland, OR.

All Scripture references are from the New International Version, unless otherwise noted.

Printed in China

New Leaf Press
A Division of New Leaf Publishing Group
www.newleafpress.net

Presented to:

_____

Presented by:

_____

Date:

_____

Day 1
Some Fathers Do

A soldier returning home from the Vietnam War got off the train with a limp and an arm in a sling. A small gray-haired woman ran to him, followed by a big man who kept up with her by simply walking faster. She embraced the boy and shed some tears. The father moved closer and stated, "I'm glad to see you, Son." Not much more was said until they reached home and the boy was in the kitchen with his mother.

"You know, Mom, I get a kick out of Pa," he said. "Did you notice him at the station? No dramatics. No frog in his throat like a lot of men would have. Of course, you understand, I know he likes me . . . I mean, he probably loves me . . . but what I mean is you'll never catch Pop losing his head. Boy, he's got ice water in his veins. What a general he would have made!"

"Son," his mother said, "he loves you very much. I know."

"Sure, I know, too. Say, where is Pop?"

"He's outside. You better run in and see how we've fixed your room."

The young man left, and she went out the back door, knowing exactly where to find her husband. She looked through the crack of the garage door and saw him on his knees. The step stool was his altar.

"I want to thank You, God," the big man was saying. "I asked You, God, to give me a break and let him come out all right, though

I knew then I didn't have any more right to ask than anybody else. But now he's back safe. So I want to thank You, God. I want to thank You very much. Amen." He rose slowly.

The woman returned to her kitchen. The young man came back saying, "The room looks swell. Say, where did Pop go?"

"He'll be right in," his mother said. "There was just something he had to do."

Many times fathers attempt to hide their real feelings. Why? Probably because in our society, men are still taught to be macho, silent, and tough.

Sir, it's okay to express how you feel. Allow yourself to be human, to show an expression, to be loving and caring.

Being a father in today's world requires the best from every man who is a father. And what about your father? Have you prayed for him lately? Have you taken the time to express thanks to him for what he has done in your life?

Today's Quote: *The head man of any family, like the head man of any business, holds importance only so long as he isn't unduly impressed with it!* — Oren Arnold

Today's Verse: As a father has compassion on his children, so the Lord has compassion on those who fear him (Ps. 103:13).

Day 2
Forgiven

A certain seminary professor always introduces his class on the New Testament with a story from his own life. As a young man he told a lie to his father and hurt him deeply. For years the matter went unresolved, but the guilt and remorse kept gnawing away at him until, finally, he wrote his father a letter.

Because he was not even sure that his father would remember, the professor reviewed the entire episode and asked his father to forgive him. A few days later he received a reply in which the father said, "Of course I remember, and of course I forgive you."

The son said it was like a great weight had fallen from his shoulders, and it made all the difference in his life. But the real payoff came several years later when both his mother and father died within a short time of each other.

As the oldest son, he went to their house and was going through their things. Up in the attic he found a box containing little treasures his parents had kept through the years from their marriage and from his childhood. As he looked through the box, his eyes welled up with tears because he felt so close to his parents and the things that had been most important to them.

Then he found the letter that he had written, asking for forgiveness. He opened it and began to read, and with tears running down his cheeks, he turned it over. And there, in his father's handwriting, was one word: "FORGIVEN!" And it was underlined.

In that moment he realized that his father had really let go of the issue that had come between them. He had written "forgiven" on the letter, then put it aside in the box of treasures because it was over. There was no unfinished business.

What a great gift it was for that son to discover that his father had relinquished all traces of the hurt and the resentment and the bitterness!

What a fantastic gift it is when we are able to forgive and let go — to forgive and forget. This is exactly the way in which God, our Heavenly Father, deals with us. When we are forgiven by God, it is as if we had never done that which caused our estrangement from Him.

Where are you in regard to forgiveness today? Do you need to forgive another, or are you in need of forgiveness yourself? God will help in both situations.

Today's Quote: *He who cannot forgive others breaks the bridge over which he must pass himself.* — George Herbert

Today's Verse: For if you forgive men when they sin against you, your heavenly Father will also forgive you. But if you do not forgive men their sins, your Father will not forgive your sins (Matt. 6:14–15).

Day 3
Foolish Heroics?

The young farmer sat happily on the wagon seat as his spirited team made their way into the little Kansas town. After hitching the team to a rack near the corner of the main street, he walked down to the general store to buy the week's supply of groceries and goods.

He had hardly entered the store when a bunch of boys came walking down the street lighting and flipping firecrackers. One of the boys flipped one directly in front of the team of horses. When the firecracker burst, the team reared and lunged against the lines holding them. The lines snapped. When the team came down, the scared animals laid back their ears and thundered down the main street.

At that moment the young farmer looked out of the store to take in the scene. Without a bit of hesitation, he threw himself into the street just as the frightened horses came by with manes flying. With a jump he managed to grab the bridle of the horse nearest to him.

The running team jerked him off his feet and dragged him down the street with them. But with an iron grip he held on, and the team began to slow down a bit. In about fifty or a hundred yards, he was able to get around in front to reach for the other bridle. But the horses wouldn't give in quite so easy and reared again. With front hooves flying, down they came. One of those deadly, flying hooves caught the farmer full in his face. Slowly that iron grip began to relax on the bridle as he slumped into the dust of the street. Other men by this time were able to get the team under control.

They carried the dead young farmer to the plank sidewalk and laid him down. One of the men spoke out of his frustration and said, "The fool! The crazy fool! Why didn't he just let them go? They would have run themselves out on the prairie. He didn't have to die like this! The crazy fool!" The rest of the men and the gathering crowd nodded in agreement. It had been a foolish kind of heroics.

Just about then they heard a sound coming from the inside the wagon box. Every person looked in that direction. Above the sideboards came the blond head of a scared little boy crying for his daddy.*

The world may look back on the sacrifice of Jesus Christ on the cross of Calvary and think it unnecessary. There is no greater demonstration of love than the giving of one's own life for another. He did it for you and me.

*John B. Wilder, *Stories for Platform* (Grand Rapids, MI: Zondervan Publishing, 1963), p. 48.

Today's Quote: *Anybody can be a heart specialist. The only requirement is loving somebody!* — Angie Papadakis

Today's Verse: For God so loved the world that he gave his one and only Son, that whoever believes in him shall not perish but have eternal life (John 3:16).

Day 4
Stolen Cookies

A small boy at a summer camp received a large package of cookies in the mail from his mother. He ate a few, then placed the remainder under his bed. The next day, after lunch, he went to his tent to get a cookie, but the box was gone.

That afternoon a camp counselor, who had been told of the theft, saw another boy sitting behind a tree eating the stolen cookies.

He returned to the group and sought out the boy whose cookies had been stolen. He said, "Billy, I know who stole your cookies. Will you help me teach him a lesson?"

The puzzled boy replied, "Well . . . yes, but aren't you going to punish him?"

The counselor explained, "No, that would make him resent me and hate you. No, I want you to call your mother and ask her to send you another box of cookies."

Billy did as the counselor asked, and a few days later received another box of delicious homemade cookies in the mail.

The counselor said, "Now, the boy who stole your cookies is down by the lake. Go down there and share your cookies with him."

The boy protested, "But, he's the thief."

"I know. But try it, and see what happens," replied the counselor.

About half an hour later, the camp counselor saw the two come up the hill, arm in arm. The boy who had stolen the cookies was earnestly trying to get the other to accept his jackknife in payment for the stolen cookies, and the victim was just as earnestly refusing the gift from his new friend, saying that a few cookies weren't important anyway.

We all have a great hunger for forgiveness as this next story indicates. It happened in Spain that a father and teenage son had a broken relationship. The son ran away, but the father searched for his rebellious son. Finally, in Madrid, in a last desperate attempt to find him, the father put an ad in the newspaper. The ad read: "Dear Paco, Meet me in front of the newspaper office at noon. All is forgiven. I love you. Your father."

The next day at noon, in front of the newspaper office, eight hundred "Pacos" showed up! It seems that all these young men with the name Paco were seeking forgiveness and love from their fathers.

Does a child of yours need your forgiveness today? Or maybe, you need to seek your father's forgiveness. Remember, God, the Father, still forgives! And so should we.

Today's Quote: *Forgiveness is a God who will not leave us after all we've done!* — George Roemisch

Today's Verse: The Lord is gracious and righteous; our God is full of compassion (Ps. 116:5).

Day 5
Just "Dad"

Father's Day, which is observed the third Sunday of each June, was not the brainchild of a group of disgruntled fathers who resented the attention given to mothers. According to the National Father's Day Committee — a volunteer organization of notables from every walk of life united to promote better father-child relationships — it was initiated on June 19, 1910, three years *before* the first official Mother's Day.

This commemoration was the idea of Mrs. John Bruce Dodd of Spokane, Washington. She had suggested the idea to honor her own father, William Smart, a veteran of the Civil War, who had reared his six motherless children on an eastern Washington farm. Smart was a widower left with these children after the birth of their sixth child. His daughter thought he had done such an outstanding job as both father and mother that she had wanted to do something to perpetuate his memory. The occasion was soon expanded to include all American fathers.

William Jennings Bryan was one of the first to give his endorsement to Mrs. Dodd's plan. Then James Whitcomb Riley wrote, "My heart is with you in this great work."

In 1924 President Calvin Coolidge was the first president to recommend the national observance of Father's Day. The original intent of this day was a dedication to the building of good citizenship at home, in the nation, and in the church. That should be a challenge to all us fathers.

When is a father just "Dad"? H.C. Chatfield answers: "If he's wealthy and prominent and you stand in awe of him, call him 'Father.' If he sits in his shirt sleeves and suspenders at ball games and picnics, call him 'Pop.' If he tills the land or labors in overalls, call him 'Pa.' If he wheels the baby carriage, call him 'Papa' with the accent on the first syllable. If, however, he makes a pal of you when you're good, and is too wise to let you pull the wool over his loving eyes when you're not; if you're sure no one else has quite so fine a father, you may call him 'Dad.' "

Today's Quote: *Fathers are the great gift-givers of the world!* — Mrs. John Bruce Dodd, founder of Father's Day

Today's Verse: "Honor your father and mother" — which is the first commandment with a promise — "that it may go well with you and that you may enjoy long life on the earth" (Eph. 6:2–3).

Father made me learn so many Bible verses every day that by the time I was 11 years of age, I had learned about three-fourths of the Old Testament and all of the New by heart.

John Muir (1838–1914)

Day 6
It Took More Grace

A large, prosperous downtown London church had three mission churches it had started under its care. On the first Sunday of the new year all the members of the mission churches came to the downtown mother church for a combined communion service. From those mission churches, which were located in the slums of the city, had come some outstanding cases of conversions — burglars, thieves, drunks, and so on. All knelt side by side at the common communion rail to share in this special service.

On this particular occasion, the pastor saw a former burglar kneeling beside a judge of the Supreme Court of England — the same judge who had sent the burglar to jail for seven years. After his release, this thief had been converted and become an excellent Christian worker in the church. Yet, as they knelt there, the judge and the former convict, neither one seemed to be aware of the other.

After the service, the pastor was walking home with the judge who said to him, "Did you notice who was kneeling beside me at the communion rail this morning?"

The pastor replied, "Yes, but I didn't know that you noticed." The two walked along in silence for a few more moments.

Then the judge said, "What a miracle of grace."

The pastor nodded, "Yes, what marvelous grace."

Then the judge said, "But to whom do you refer?"

And the pastor said, "Why, to the conversion of that convict."

The judge said, "I don't refer to him. I was thinking of myself."

Now the pastor turned in surprise, "You were thinking of yourself? I guess I don't understand."

"Yes," the judge replied, "it did not cost that burglar much to get converted when he came out of jail. He had nothing but a history of crime behind him. When he saw Jesus as his Saviour, he knew there was salvation and hope for him. And he knew how much he needed that help. But look at me. I was taught from infancy to live as a gentleman; that my word was my bond; that I was to say my prayers, go to church, take communion, and so on. I went through Oxford, earned my degrees, was called to the bar, and eventually became a judge. Pastor, nothing but the grace of God could have caused me to admit that I was a sinner on a level with that burglar. It took more grace."

Today's Quote: *The grace of God is unmerited love to man in the form of Jesus Christ!* — Unknown

Today's Verse: For it is by grace you have been saved, through faith — and this not from yourselves, it is the gift of God — not by works, so that no one can boast (Eph. 2:8–9).

Day 7
Forgiving Father

On a cold winter evening a man suffered a heart attack and was admitted to the hospital. After being treated in the emergency room and taken to his room for the stay, he asked the nurse if she would please call his daughter. He explained, "You see, I live alone, and she is the only family I have."

The nurse went to phone the daughter. The nurse was immediately aware that the daughter was quite upset. As she almost shouted into the phone, the daughter said, "You must not let him die! You see, Dad and I had a terrible argument almost a year ago. I haven't seen him since. All these months, I've wanted to go to him for forgiveness. The last thing I said to him was 'I hate you.' "

There was a pause, then crying on the daughter's end. Then through the tears, "I'm coming now, I'll be there in about 30 minutes."

In the meantime, the patient slipped into cardiac arrest, and an alert was sounded. The nurse who made the phone call prayed, "Oh God, his daughter is on her way. Don't let it end like this."

The efforts of the medical team to revive the patient were fruitless. They had administered adrenaline, then attempted to shock the heart into action but to no avail. The patient died.

The nurse then noticed one of the doctors talking to the daughter outside the room. She could see the pathetic look on the woman's face and read the hurt that had surfaced. The nurse then stepped in, took the young lady aside, and said, "I'm so sorry."

The daughter responded, "I never hated him, you know. I loved him. And now I want to go in and see him."

The nurse thought, *Why put yourself through more pain?* But she took the young woman into the room. The daughter went to the bed and buried her face in the sheets as she sobbed her goodbye to her now deceased father.

The nurse, as she tried not to look at the sad farewell, noticed a scrap of paper on the table by the bed. She picked it up, read it, and then handed it to the distraught daughter. It read: "My dearest Donna, I do forgive you. I pray you will also forgive me. I know that you love me. I love you, too." And it was signed, "Daddy."

The tragedy of guilt and what could have been all come to mind. How much better if forgiveness had been offered sooner. Don't wait!

Today's Quote: *Forgiveness is man's deepest need and God's highest achievement!* — Horace Bushnell

Today's Verse: And when you stand praying, if you hold anything against anyone, forgive him, so that your Father in heaven may forgive you your sins (Mark 11:25;TEV).

Day 8
Send Us the Money!

Shortly after the Dallas Theological Seminary was founded in 1924 it nearly went under. In fact, the school came to the very point of bankruptcy and teetered on the edge. The creditors were planning to foreclose at noon on this particular day, in spite of the fact that everything humanly possible had been tried to raise the needed money.

On this morning of doomsday, many of the faculty and board members met in the president's office with Dr. Chafer to pray that God would somehow provide the miracle of finance. As is the custom in Baptist circles, a prayer circle was formed, and each man prayed in turn.

Among those present was Dr. Harry Ironside. When it was his turn, he prayed in his characteristic to-the-point manner: "Lord, we know that the cattle on a thousand hills are Thine. Please sell some of them and send us the money." When completed, the next person prayed, and they continued on around this very concerned group of men.

While they were in their prayer meeting, a tall Texan with boots, jeans, and an open collared shirt walked into the business office and said to the receptionist, "I just sold two carloads of cattle in Fort Worth. I've been trying to make a business deal go through, and it won't work. Now I feel compelled to give the money to the seminary. I don't know if you need it or not, but here's the check!"

The little secretary reached for the check and looked at the amount. Aware of the critical nature of the situation, she immediately got up and headed in the direction of the prayer meeting. Knocking timidly, she did not want to disturb the prayers but needed to get somebody's attention. She kept on tapping until finally, the president, Dr. Chafer, went to the door.

With great excitement, she explained what had happened and handed him the check. Dr. Chafer took the check from her hand and noticed it was made out in exactly the amount for which they had been praying. He then examined the name on the check and recognized it as the cattleman from Forth Worth. Turning around, he re-entered the circle and interrupted one of the men in mid-prayer. Turing to Dr. Harry Ironside, he almost shouted in his excitement, "Harry, God sold the cattle!"

Today, you may be hurting in a financial way. You may be questioning God and His provision. Keep on praying. God still cares and He still provides!

Today's Quote: *To pray is the greatest thing we can do, and to do it well, there must be calmness, time, and deliberation!* — E.M. Bounds

Today's Verse: And my God will meet all your needs according to his glorious riches in Christ Jesus (Phil. 4:19).

Day 9
There's a Reason

Lou Little, the former great football coach at Columbia University, relates the following story.

This particular season the team had played through the schedule without a defeat. Now they were facing the final game of the year, and the Ivy League Conference Championship was on the line. It was winner take all. Their opponent was arch rival Harvard, also undefeated.

On Tuesday of the week in which preparation was being made, Coach Little received a phone call asking him if he would break the tragic news to one of his players that the boy's father had died and the funeral was to be on Friday. The young man was a senior on the football squad, and an unusual young man. Although he had never started a game in his four-year career, the boy had been kept on the team because of his irrepressible and contagious attitude. He was an inspiration.

After the coach called him aside and broke the news, the young man immediately left and told the coach, "I'll be back in time for the big game on Saturday."

Coach Little replied, "Son, take as much time with your family as you need. We'll just go with the team that has won so far. Don't worry."

The day of the big game arrived, and the young man, as he had promised, suited up with the rest of the team. He went over to the coach and said, "Lou, please let me start this game — even one play!" The coach kind of brushed him aside, but the young man was emotionally insistent and came back with his request again, "Please, Coach, even one play!" So Lou agreed to let him start.

Columbia won the toss and elected to kick-off. This young man was the first tackler down field and tackled the ball carrier on the seven-yard line. A great play. On the first play from scrimmage, the Harvard quarterback called for the halfback to go over his slot. The young man tackled him on the five-yard line for a two-yard loss. The next play the Harvard quarterback dropped into the end zone to pass, and this young man tackled him, scoring a safety. He played the entire game.

After the game, Little asked, "Son, what got into you today?"

The young man replied, with tears in his eyes, "Coach, do you remember that my father was blind? Today is the first time he's seen me play!"

Today's Quote: *Life demands the best effort because we are all playing on the field of life under the all seeing eye of a kind, loving Heavenly Father!* — Unknown

Today's Verse: Brothers, I do not consider myself yet to have taken hold of it. But one thing I do: Forgetting what is behind and straining toward what is ahead, I press on toward the goal to win the prize (Phil. 3:13–14).

What Price Freedom?

Have you ever wondered what happened to those brave men who signed the document we call the "Declaration of Independence"?

Five signers were captured by the British as traitors and tortured before they were executed. Twelve had their homes ransacked and burned. Two lost their sons in the Revolutionary War; another had two sons captured. Nine of the 56 fought and died from wounds or the hardships of the Revolution.*

What kind of men were they? Twenty-four were lawyers, 11 were merchants, 9 were farmers or plantation owners. Most were men of means and well-educated. Yet they signed this document knowing full well that the penalty would be death or worse if captured.

They pledged: "For the support of this declaration, with a firm reliance on the protection of the Divine Providence, we mutually pledge to each other our lives, our fortunes, and our sacred honor."

Carter Baxton of Virginia, a wealthy trader, saw his ships swept from the seas by the British navy. He sold his home and properties to pay his debts and died in rags.

Thomas McKeam was so hounded by the British that he was forced to move his family constantly. He served in the Congress without pay, and his family was kept in hiding. Eventually, his possessions were taken from him, and poverty overtook him.

Vandals or soldiers or both looted the properties of Ellery, Clymer, Hall, Walton, Gwinnett, Heyward, Ruttledge, and Middleton.

At the Battle of Yorktown, Thomas Nelson Jr. noted that British General Cornwallis had taken over the Nelson home for his headquarters. The owner quietly urged General George Washington to open fire, which was done. The home was destroyed and Nelson died bankrupt.

Francis Lewis had his home and properties destroyed. The enemy jailed his wife and she died in a few short months.

John Hart was driven from his wife's bedside as she was dying; their children fled for their lives. Hart's fields and mill were laid waste. He died from exhaustion and a broken heart.

Norris and Livingston suffered the same fates.

And such are the stories of the American Revolution. These were not wild-eyed, rabble-rousing ruffians; these were men of means. They had security, but they valued liberty more. They may have lost their lives and fortunes, but their sacred honor is preserved today in the hearts and minds of all freedom loving people throughout the world.

Today's Quote: *Whatever makes men good Christians makes them good citizens!* — Daniel Webster

Today's Verse: Blessed is the nation whose God is the Lord (Ps. 33:12).

Day 11
Strike Out

It was the fourth game of the 1954 World Series. The stands were buzzing. One more out and the New York Giants would beat the Cleveland Indians four games in a row.

The Cleveland batter hit a lazy pop fly that drifted across the third base foul line. Bill Bailey (not his real name) came running under, reached up, and grabbed it. Fellow Giants swarmed on the field to smother him with congratulations.

Not only had Bill made the last out, but he had hit in every game, batting .364 and breaking a World Series record with seven walks in four games.

Bill kept the ball of the final out as a memento of the series. But he doesn't have it now. Rules about personal property are strict in the Texas pen where he served a ten-year term for armed robbery.

Bill got only $90 from the liquor store robbery. His share of the 1954 World Series came to $11,000 (a lot in those days), and he made at least another quarter million from product endorsements.

How does a guy go from a World Series hero to a convict in less than ten years? "Liquor and bad friends," Bill told a reporter.

When Bill was a baseball player and was loaded with money, he had an infield-full of friends. They cheered Bill when he picked up the checks in restaurants and night clubs.

Players remember Bill as a "great guy with charm, except when he hit the booze." After Bill was dropped from baseball, he became a bartender. When his money ran out, he would return to the ballpark to borrow money off his former teammates. "I'm gonna get a hit pretty soon," he would tell them. "I'm gonna quit striking out."

But Bill Bailey never got his "break." Liquor and bad friends kept throwing him curves, until one day the ex-hero took a final bad pitch and was handed a prison sentence. That day none of his friends were around to see him strike out.

Today we don't know the outcome of Bill Bailey. The only thing that remains is his name on some old score books to let us know that at one time he was a major league ballplayer.

Life is much more than a game, but it's still up to us to play by the rules. In the Bible, God has carefully laid out the guidelines for a successful life. If you want to hit a home run, make sure you're on the right playing field.

Today's Quote: *It matters not that you won or lost, but how you played the game!* — Unknown

Today's Verse: Beware, the Lord is about to take firm hold of you and hurl you away, O you mighty man. He will roll you up tightly like a ball and throw you into a large country (Isa. 22:17–18).

Day 12
Foundational Note

A shepherd living up in the hills of Idaho was a faithful listener to one of the finer musical programs that originated from a radio station in Los Angeles each Sunday night. One evening after listening to the concert of classical music, he wrote a letter to the radio station with a most unusual request. The letter said in part, "I enjoy your program every week, and I'm writing to ask you a favor. It's rather lonely up here in the hills, and I haven't much to entertain me except listening to the radio. I have an old violin, which I once could play, but it has gotten badly out of tune. I wonder if you would take just a moment on your program next week to strike "A" on the piano so that I may tune my violin again."

At first they smiled about the letter, but then the station decided to honor the request. The following Sunday night when the program came on the air they interrupted it long enough to strike "A" on the studio piano in Los Angeles while the shepherd out in the hills of Idaho got the right pitch for his violin.

That's a great little story. Why? This world of ours is badly out of tune. We need a Higher Power to strike the right note, a foundational note, to give us the right pitch for our lives and living.

It was almost two thousand years ago, in a little-known corner of the world called Palestine, that God "in the fullness of time" sounded the master note upon the instruments of heaven.

Jesus Christ of Nazareth, the Son of Man and the Son of God, was that master note. He was the "A" sounded that men might tune their lives to Him and in doing so find the answer to life and the meaning of life. Have you let Him strike "A" in your life? No matter what the discord — no matter how far off-key your life has gotten — He can turn your life into the symphony God intended it to be.

Life may prove to be harsh and difficult. Life may deny you your dreams and starve your precious hopes. Life may have taken from you that which you considered most precious. Life may have turned fickle and unpredictable. But in Jesus Christ there is an answer! He is the basic foundation on which you can build or rebuild your life. Let Him strike "A" in your life!

Today's Quote: *Settle one difficulty and you keep a hundred others away!* — Chinese Proverb

Today's Verse: Then Peter said, "Silver and gold I do not have, but what I have I give you" (Acts 3:6).

My father was a Methodist and believed in the laying on of hands, and believe me, he really laid them on!

A.W. Tozer (1897–1963)

Day 13
Belief

A world famous bird watcher had seen every bird in the United States except one that lived in the mountains of Colorado, so he traveled to the mountains to find this rare bird. After a couple of days of searching, he finally spotted it and immediately became fixed on the size and beauty of the creature. He started to walk in the direction of the rare beauty, forgetting he was near the edge of a cliff. Sure enough, he walked off the edge, but as he was tumbling down he hit a small tree and was able to grab on. He was dangling 100 feet from the top and 1,000 feet from the bottom.

He cried for help and heard a reassuring voice say, "I'm here."

The man was thrilled that someone had heard him, and he asked, "Who are you?"

The voice replied, "I am the Lord."

The man said, "I am *sooo* glad You came along. I can't hold on much longer."

The voice said, "Before I help you, I want to know if you believe in Me."

The man answered, "Lord, I certainly believe in You. I go to church every Sunday, sometimes even on Wednesday. I read my Bible at least once a week, even though I don't understand it. I pray at least every other day, and I even put a few dollars in the offering plate."

The voice replied, "But do you really believe in Me?"

The man was getting more desperate. "Lord, You can't believe how much I believe in You. I am 100 percent committed to You. I believe totally in what You say. I BELIEVE!"

The Lord said, "Good. Now let go of the branch!"

The man stammered, "But Lord. . . ."

The voice of the Lord came back, "If you believe in Me, let go of the branch."

The man was silent for a minute, and then he yells, "Is anybody else up there?"

Belief is not belief until it is translated into action! Whoever said that an exercise of faith would be easy? Head games are not belief.

Faith is a substance. It becomes a reality when it is put into action. The other Apostles said they believed in Jesus Christ, but it was only the apostle Peter who walked on water. Yes, I know he got wet in the process, but his action translated into a peerless walk!

Today's Quote: *Confidence . . . is entering a sales contest and wondering who's going to come in second!* — Paul Ziegler

Today's Verse: But without faith it is impossible to please him: for he that cometh to God must believe that he is, and that he is a rewarder of them that diligently seek him (Heb. 11:6;KJV).

Day 14
Thy Father Seeketh Thee

A Quaker family lived in Pennsylvania. Against the father's wishes, his son Jonathan ran off and enlisted in the cause of the North during the Civil War. Time passed, and no word came from Jonathan. One night the father had a dream that his son had been wounded in action, was in distress, and needed the care of his father.

The father left the farm and attempted to discover where the troops might be camped. Making his way by horse-drawn buggy, he came to the scene of action. He inquired until he found the commander and asked about his son. The commander replied that there had been heavy action earlier in the day, and many had fallen wounded. Some had been cared for; others were still out in the trenches. Pointing in the direction of where the fighting had taken place, he gave permission to the father to go and try to find his son.

It was now dusk, and the father lit a lantern. While searching for his son, he came across many wounded young men. Some were calling for help, and others were too seriously wounded to cry for assistance.

The task seemed impossible. How could he find his son among all those wounded and dying? He devised a little plan. Methodically, he would comb the scene of action with his lantern. But that wasn't fruitful as he stumbled over body after body.

Then he began calling loudly as he walked, "Jonathan Smythe, thy father seeketh after thee!" He would walk a little ways and call again, "Jonathan Smythe, thy father seeketh thee. . . ." A groan and response could be heard here and there, "I wish that were my father."

He kept diligently at his search. Then, he heard a very faint, barely audible reply, "Father, over here." And as the father approached closer — "I knew you would come."

The father knelt down, took his son into his arms, comforted him with his presence, gave him some water to drink, dressed the wound, carried him to the buggy, and took him to a place of seclusion to nurse him back to health.

It reminds me of another father with a wayward son whose story Jesus told us in the Bible (Luke 15). This in turn reminds me of our loving kind Heavenly Father who is constantly on the lookout for His hurting, wounded, lost children.

My friend, if as you read this, you are one of those lost ones, I assure you that the Heavenly Father is only an invitation away!

Today's Quote: *A man should be ashamed to run his own life the minute he finds out there is a God!* — Paul Radar

Today's Verse: Cast all your anxiety on him because he cares for you (1 Pet. 5:7).

Day 15
Pillars

Famed English architect Sir Christopher Wren designed a large dome for a church that was so unique he became the object of much criticism among his colleagues. During the construction of this dome, his critics created so much fuss the authorities demanded that Wren add two huge supporting pillars to keep the dome from collapsing. Wren bitterly objected, insisting on the strength of his structure and the wisdom of his new architectural innovation. Besides, it would ruin the beauty and aesthetics of the church. But the opposition was well-organized and powerful. The two pillars were added to the design over Wren's objections.

Fifty years passed since the construction of the controversial dome. It was now time to repaint the interior of the church, as well as the dome.

When the painters erected their scaffolding to begin the painting, they made the startling discovery that the two added pillars did not even touch the dome! They were short by two feet!

Sir Christopher Wren had such confidence in his work that he made sure the offending pillars were freestanding. The authorities, during his lifetime, had made their inspection from the floor, seen the pillars, and assumed they reached the roof. They now felt secure, even though the pillars didn't support anything! Wren went to his grave with his little secret well-kept. I believe he may have had the last laugh!

Man has built many pillars to support his little world and to keep things from falling in on him. They may seem strong and able to stand the stress of time, but often they are just as useless as architect Wren's false columns.

Some have constructed pillars of religion, beautiful in structure and firm in appearance. But religion is totally meaningless without the person of Jesus Christ. Pillars of religion are freestanding and have no hold on eternity.

Others have erected pillars of intellectualism, money, pleasure, or philosophy. Lest we despair, there is a structure that is ample for the ultimate crisis of life. As Wren had confidence in his architectural creation, so can you have confidence in the structure God builds in your life!

Today's Quote: *Christ is not valued at all unless He is valued above all!* — Augustine

Today's Verse: I am sending Christ to be the carefully chosen, precious Cornerstone of my church, and I will never disappoint those who trust in him (1 Pet. 2:6;LB).

Day 16
Addicted to Activity

"See how they run, see how they run, they all run after . . ." duties, assignments, appointments, demands, deadlines! There are plans, programs, and people, so run, run, run!

How about taking a moment to sit down, let your motor idle, and take another sip from your coffee cup? Think about your pace. Are you part of the rat race? How did you get trapped? Are you being fulfilled?

James Sullivan knows exactly how you feel. Back in the sixties he blew Oklahoma City wide open, developing the world's largest "Young Life Club" — a Christian group for young people. But that's not all he blew apart. In doing it, he sacrificed his family and his health. He was a very hard man to keep up with, let alone live with.

His wife and family were tired. Life lived at full-bore was, in reality, an escape technique. He wrote the book *The Frog Who Never Became a Prince,* and we lift one line from it. "I was a man who existed in a shell . . . guilt, resentment, and hatred welled up within me. The resulting hard feeling I developed became almost insurmountable."

Wasn't James Sullivan working for Jesus Christ and the kingdom of God? Yes, but he substituted activity for living.

One Thanksgiving Day his wife, Carolyn, asked him a question as he was once more racing out the door to speak at a youth meeting,

"Do you know, or do you even care, that from the middle of September until today you have not been home one night?" Not very long after that incident, she broke emotionally, while he contemplated suicide.

Does this story sound familiar? There are many churches in our land that boast, "Something every night of the week for everybody!" What a shame, and it's even worse that churches advertise it.

God's Word speaks often and loudly about cultivating a calm, peaceful inner spirit. Instead, we offer Him a life full of activity, noise, and more and more running! Could the reason we run so much be to deaden the pain of an empty life?

To change this activity, I suggest you start with admitting you are too busy; then learn the art of saying a small two letter word, "NO" — and mean it. It may take some practice. All together now, let's say it again — "NO!" And keep on saying no! There are a lot of us who are addicted to activity who would like to stop if we could. Do it before it's too late — for the sake of your wife, your children, and your relationship to God.

Today's Quote: *The stops of a good man are ordered by the Lord as well as his steps!* — George Mueller

Today's Verse: "Be still, and know that I am God; I will be exalted among the nations, I will be exalted in the earth" (Ps. 46:10).

Day 17
Old Hickory

He's called "Old Hickory" because of his grit! His mother named him Andrew on March 15, 1767, when she gave birth to this independent rebel. He was not interested in school. He was wild, quick-tempered, and answered the call for soldiers at age 13.

Shortly after becoming a soldier, he was taken prisoner. While a captive, he refused to polish an enemy officer's boots and was struck with a saber. This was Andrew's first introduction to pain.

He carried that mark for the rest of his life, but his disposition never changed. Andrew was a fighter to the core. He chose to settle arguments in duels and lived most of his life with two bullets painfully lodged in his body.

After his battlefield heroics, his name became a household word for courage. When politics called, "Old Hickory" accepted the challenge. He was voted to the United States Senate, then there was the nomination for the presidency. It was then he experienced a different kind of pain — he lost a narrow race to Quincy Adams.

Four years later, Andrew ran again and won! But two months before he was to take the oath of office, he lost his beloved wife, Rachel. Grief-stricken and ill, the president-elect carried on and was sworn in as our seventh president as he fought the raging fever caused by an abscess in his lung. Later, one of the bullets in his body was surgically removed — without benefit of an anesthetic!

Even his political career was painful at times. A nasty scandal split his cabinet, allowing critics to have a field day at his expense. However, he weathered that storm and was one of the very few presidents to leave the office more popular than when he came.

I believe it was pain that drew the qualities of greatness out of Andrew Jackson! Pain can humble the proud; it can soften the stubborn; it can melt the hard; and the heart alone knows its own sorrow. This message can be communicated to statesmen, presidents, servants, preachers, and prodigals. By staying, pain refuses to be ignored; and by hurting, it reduces the victim to anguish. It's at this point that the sufferer submits and learns. Here is developed either maturity of character or self-pity of soul. Every strong-willed person who has become great knows the meaning of pain.

Today's Quote: *No man can be brave who thinks pain the greatest evil; nor temperate, who considers pleasure the highest good!* — Cicero

Today's Verse: He said unto me, "My grace is sufficient for you, for my power is made perfect in weakness." Therefore I will boast all the more gladly about my weaknesses, so that Christ's power may rest on me (2 Cor. 12:9).

Day 18
Staying in Touch

Back in the days when New Bedford, Massachusetts, was a major seaport, scores of ships involved in the whaling industry went out from it each year. They covered all the seas and often spent many years away from their home base. Of all the captains made famous for their seamanship, none was more highly regarded than Elieazar Hall. He went further, stayed out longer, brought back more whale oil, and lost fewer men than anyone else.

Captain Hall had little formal education and had learned all that he knew by sailing. When asked about his almost uncanny gift in navigation, his ability to know just where he was and how to get where he wanted to go, Captain Hall would answer in this way: "Oh, I just go up on the deck; I listen to the wind in the rigging; I get the drift of the sea; I take a long look at the stars; and then I set my course."

Well, times changed, and the owners of Captain Hall's vessel were informed that the insurance underwriters would no longer agree to cover a vessel that did not carry a formally trained and certified navigator. They were then confronted with the problem of how to break the news to Captain Hall. He must either sign on some youngster or go to navigation school himself. The directors of the company drew straws, and finally one was assigned the dreadful task of breaking the news to the salty sea captain. But to everyone's astonishment, Captain Hall greeted the announcement with no particular emotion. Since he had always been curious about this new business of scientific navigation, he was glad for the opportunity to study it.

At the expense of the company, he went to navigation school and graduated near the top of his class. Then he shipped out for two years on the high seas. The day Captain Hall returned to port after his first voyage, half of the marine population of New Bedford was on the docks to greet him. And, of course, the first question asked was how he enjoyed the experience of navigation by scientific means.

He said, "It was wonderful. I don't know how I have gotten on without it all these years. Whenever I wanted to know my location, I would go into my cabin, get out my charts and tables, work the proper equations, and set my course with scientific precision. I would then go up on the deck, and I would listen to the wind in the rigging. I'd get the drift of the sea, and I would take a long look at the stars. Then I would go back and correct my errors in computation."

Today's Quote: *If you would have God's guidance, you must listen as well as talk to the Guide!* — Eld

Today's Verse: In all your ways acknowledge him, and he will make your paths straight (Prov. 3:6).

Day 19
The Empty Chair

Leslie Weatherhead tells the story of an old Scotsman who was quite ill. The family called for their "Domini," or minister. As the minister entered the sick room and sat down, he noticed that another chair on the opposite side of the bed had also been drawn up close.

The pastor said, "Don, I see I'm not your first visitor for the day."

The old man looked up, was puzzled for a moment, then recognized from the nod of the head that the pastor had noticed the empty chair. "Well, Pastor, I'll tell you about that chair. Many years ago I found it quite difficult to pray, so one day I shared this problem with my pastor. He told me not to worry about kneeling or about placing myself in some pious position. Instead he said, 'Just sit down, put a chair opposite you, and imagine Jesus sitting in it; then talk with Him as you would a friend.'" The aged old Scotsman then added, "I've been doing that ever since."

A short time later the daughter of the Scot called the minister once again. When he answered, she informed him that her father had died very suddenly. She was quite shaken for she had no idea death was so near. Then she continued, "I had just gone to lie down for an hour or two because he seemed to be sleeping so comfortably. When I went back, he was dead." Then she added thoughtfully, "Except now his hand was on the empty chair at the side of the bed. Isn't that strange?"

The minister said, "No, it's not so strange. I understand."

For all of us, prayer and the presence of Jesus must be as near and real as it was with this old Scot. In our mind we understand that, yes, Jesus Christ is near and real and that He hears us when we pray. But too often we act like He is such a great distance removed from us that we cannot reach Him in our times of need.

One of these days, all of us will have to face the reality of death. In that moment, you must move forward whether you want to or not. What a comfort it will be to reach out and place your hand into His and pass into eternity with Jesus!

Today's Quote: *It is more important to know where you are going than to see how fast you can get there!* — Martin Vanbee

Today's Verse: For what is your life? It is even a vapor, that appeareth for a little time, and then vanisheth away (James 4:14;KJV).

I'm left with the memory of a child who said with his eyes, "Could you be a daddy to me?"

James C. Dobson (1936–)

Who Is Handicapped?

Arnold Palmer was once invited to speak to a convention of blind golfers. (This story has many versions, so the truth cannot be absolutely guaranteed.) He asked them how they were able to know what direction to hit the ball. One blind golfer explained that the caddie went on ahead of him with a little bell, which he would ring as he stood near the hole. The blind golfer would then hit the ball toward the sound of the bell.

Arnold asked how well it worked, and the blind golfer said that it worked so well he was willing to take on Palmer for a round of golf! Just to make it interesting, he was willing to bet Palmer $10,000 he could beat him. That just blew Palmer's mind! Ten thousand dollars!

Palmer was a bit hesitant, so this blind golfer pushed him by saying, "What's the matter, are you afraid to play a blind golfer?"

So the deal was struck. Palmer said, "When do we tee off?"

And the blind golfer said, "Tonight at 11:30!" Under this set of circumstances, I don't know if I'd call that a handicap, but handicaps come in all sizes, and they can be mental just as well.

In the country church of a small village, an altar boy serving the priest at Sunday mass accidentally dropped the cruet of wine. The village priest struck the altar boy sharply on the cheek and in a gruff voice shouted, "Leave the altar and don't come back!"

The altar boy grew up — his name was Tito, the Communist leader!

In the cathedral of a large city, an altar boy serving the bishop at Sunday mass accidentally dropped the cruet of wine. With a warm twinkle in his eyes, the bishop gently whispered, "Someday you will be a priest."

That boy grew up to become the late Archbishop Fulton J. Sheen.

Think of the fantastic power of words. This is not to say that the entire life pattern for these men was set by the incident at the altar. Much more goes into making a life, but it is true that life can turn on a hinge of words spoken. With the words we speak, we can add to the burden of life or lift the cares from the shoulders of another. Handicapping often occurs because we have allowed others to dictate our future or, by our own words, have hindered those to whom we speak. The blind golfer had worked to overcome his handicap and, in fact, turned it to an advantage.

How about lifting someone's burden today with a kind, encouraging word? Who knows whom you may be talking to!

Today's Quote: *Success is never sure, and failure is never final!* — Unknown

Today's Verse: The thief comes only to steal and kill and destroy; I have come that they may have life, and have it to the full (John 10:10).

Day 21
The Great Unknown

San Francisco has had more than its share of colorful characters. Among those of the last century was a strikingly handsome man who was called the "Great Unknown." He was tall, erect, slender, with jet black hair, and was clean-shaven at a time when most men wore beards or mustaches. His dress was absolutely impeccable. He wore a top hat that was always brushed and clean. His boots were always polished. He was aloof, mysterious, and never talked with anyone. Nobody knew his name, his origin, his occupation, or where he lived. Rumor had it that he was an exiled nobleman or former diplomat, but no one knew.

One day he was missed from his normal afternoon appearance in the downtown district. His habit was to walk through the downtown district for about two hours each evening and then disappear.

Some days later, his body was found in a tiny loft by the waterfront. He lived humbly, and it was discovered that he made his living by stuffing pillows and mattresses. The room was sparse but absolutely clean.

His clothing was still immaculate. His boots were arranged in military fashion. On his dressing table was a wig of jet black hair. On the crude bed was the body, his handsome face frozen by death. His hair and beard were snow white. Whatever his secret, it died with him and he remained the "Great Unknown." He was buried in a pauper's grave with no one claiming the body.

Why? Did he attempt to be somebody he was not? Was he afraid that people might reject him as a pillow stuffer? Did he have some deep, dark, ugly secret about his past that he wanted to keep hidden? Did he crave recognition?

All of us want to be accepted and admired, but we know ourselves better than anyone else. How many of us have lived a deception? How many of us have secrets we'd rather keep to ourselves?

Jesus Christ came to set us free from deception! He came to make us sons and daughters of the King. No longer are we slaves to the past or servants to a secret. We have been accepted by Jesus Christ himself! For the first time we can look at others without suspicion or fear or deception or defense. In Christ we can be free to love and experience the great joy of living that comes from a clean conscience!

Today's Quote: *Humanity is never so beautiful as when praying for forgiveness, or else forgiving another!* — Jean Paul Richter

Today's Verse: Know ye that the Lord he is God: it is he that hath made us, and not we ourselves; we are his people, and the sheep of his pasture (Ps. 100:3;KJV).

Day 22
Abraham Lincoln's Creed

Abraham Lincoln, born in a log cabin in Kentucky on February 12, 1809, obtained his elementary education by the light of the fireplace. Later, he worked at the hardest type of labor as a farm hand and rail splitter. In 1834, he was elected to the Illinois Legislature. He became an able lawyer, and in 1846 was elected to Congress.

Although efforts to become a United States senator ended in defeat, he was elected president in 1860 and re-elected in 1864. On April 14, 1865, Lincoln was shot by an assassin and died the next day.

Many people consider Abraham Lincoln the greatest man of the nineteenth century. He rose from lowly beginnings to the highest office; led our republic through a crisis that might have destroyed it; and left a mighty heritage of kindliness, idealism, and political wisdom.

Here are a few quotes attributed to the man:

I remember a good story when I hear it, but I never invented anything original; I am only a retail dealer.

Let the people know the truth and the country is safe.

I don't think much of a man who is not wiser today than he was yesterday.

What constitutes the bulwark of our own liberty and independence? It is not our frowning battlements, our bristling seacoasts. Our reliance is in the love of liberty which God has planted in us. Our defense is in the spirit which prizes liberty, in all lands everywhere.

Let us have faith that right makes might; and in that faith let us to the end dare to do our duty as we understand it.

One thing is very significant thing about Lincoln: To this day there is still an intense curiosity about how he lived his life, how he handled his disappointments, and how he overcame difficulties.

We look for the secret of Lincoln's life and the impact it has had on forming our nation's history. For that answer we turn to his creed and discover it to have included these statements: "I believe in God, the Almighty Ruler of nations, our great and good and merciful Maker, our Father in heaven, who notes the fall of a sparrow and numbers the hairs of our heads. I believe in His eternal truth and justice."

Abraham Lincoln lived it as he wrote it.*

*E. Paul Hovey, *Treasury for Special Days (Fleming H. Revell: Westwood, NJ, 1961)*.

Today's Quote: *I have been driven many times to my knees by the overwhelming conviction that I had nowhere else to go!* — Abraham Lincoln

Today's Verse: For the Lord knoweth the way of the righteous: but the way of the ungodly shall perish (Ps. 1:6;KJV).

Day 23
Train Number 8017

Train Number 8017 wound its way through Salerno, Italy, without anyone giving a thought to the disaster its passengers faced in a few short hours on a rainy evening on March 2, 1944. The train did not collide with anything nor was it derailed, burned, or damaged in any way. Yet it brought death to more people than any other rail disaster in history. What happened?

The silent killer in this train was the low grade coal used to fire the locomotives. Shortly after 1:00 a.m. the heavy train with 600 passengers lumbered into the tunnel called "Galleria delle Armi." What went wrong nobody really knows.

When the two locomotives pulling the train reached mid-tunnel, the drive wheels apparently began to slip. Sand was then sprayed on the tracks, but that didn't help. The wheels lost traction, and the train stopped. All else is speculation as both engineers died at the controls. Carbon monoxide snuffed out more than 500 lives.

Ironically, when authorities began clearing out the bodies, they found the leading locomotive was unbraked with its controls set in reverse. The second engine was unbraked with its throttle full speed ahead! Apparently when the train stopped, the two engineers had different ideas about what to do — it proved fatal. They were pulling and pushing against each other. It was believed that if they had both been clear in their direction, either front or back, that all the passengers would have survived! But there they were, straining against each other and filling the tunnel with deadly poison.

Powerful forces are at work in our lives! We, too, have two engineers vying for direction. Lusts pull one way, our conscience the other. Intellectualism tugs at our minds; our spirits draw us toward God.

How often in our frustration have we felt that we really were opposing ourselves? Many times we come to a stop until we can sort out which direction to move. Real freedom to move in the right direction comes in your life when Christ is invited — not to take sides — but to take over.

In our world of increasing tension, it is reassuring to know that Christ can control the individual. He can help us bring these inner wars to a cease-fire. When we relinquish the controls of our living to Him, His terms of peace are always on our side.

Today's Quote: *One who knows by the assurance of the witnessing spirit that he is born of God, knows he must be free!* — Bishop Warren Candler

Today's Verse: In all these things we are more than conquerors through him that loved us (Rom. 8:37;KJV).

Day 24
The Fantastic Catch

One spring some time before the Civil War, a young man in search of work came to Worthy Taylor's prosperous Ohio farm. The farmer knew nothing much about the young man except that his name was Jim. Still he gave him a job for the summer.

Jim spent the summer cutting wood for the stove and fireplace, milking the cows, putting up hay, helping with the harvest, and anything else Mr. Taylor asked him to do. He ate in the kitchen and slept in the haymow.

Before the summer was over, Jim had fallen in love with Taylor's daughter. The farmer refused to let him marry her, telling Jim bluntly that he had no money, no name, no job, no vocation, and the prospects for his future and the future of his daughter, if married to him, were poor indeed. So the farmer said "NO" emphatically.

Jim got the message. Sadly he packed his few belongings into his old carpetbag and went on his way, never to be heard from again by the farmer or his daughter.

Thirty-five years passed, and the farmer Taylor decided to tear down his old barn to make way for a new and larger barn. When they got to removing the rafters above the old haymow, he discovered that Jim had carved his full name in one of the beams. That name was James A. Garfield. He was now the president of the United States of America!

Farmer Worthy Taylor missed the finest catch for his daughter that she could have had. The problem was compounded by the fact that Taylor's daughter had indeed married a man with his permission and blessing. Now 30 years of heartbreak had proven the husband to be a no-good bum!

Have you ever been offered a "fantastic catch" only to have turned down the opportunity? What compounds the situation is to have lived long enough to regret that mistake in judgment or choice.

Jesus Christ offers the most fantastic catch anyone can ever make — the opportunity to accept Him as Lord and personal Saviour! That decision can develop into the most exciting and growing relationship any human being could ever have.

How about you? Have you taken this step of faith? How about family members, friends, relatives, or neighbors? Farmer Taylor lived to regret his hasty decision. Don't you leave this life with regrets.

Today's Quote: *I have lived in this world just long enough to look carefully the second time into things I am the most certain of the first time!* — Josh Billings

Today's Verse: How shall we escape if we ignore such a great salvation? This salvation, which was first announced by the Lord, was confirmed to us by those who heard him (Heb. 2:3).

Day 25
It's Who You Know

During the Civil War, a young soldier walking over a battlefield came across a dear friend who was shot. His life was draining rapidly away. The soldier straightened out the shattered limb, washed the blood from his fallen comrade's face, and made him as comfortable as possible under difficult circumstances. He then said he would stay with his friend as long as life was still there. Then he asked if there was anything more he might do.

"Yes," replied the dying soldier, "if you have a piece of paper, I will dictate a note to my father, and I think I can still sign it. My father is a prominent judge in the North, and if you take him this message he will help you."

The note read, "Dear Father, I am dying on the battlefield; one of my best friends is helping me and has done his best for me. If he ever comes to you, be kind to him for your son Charlie's sake." Then with rapidly stiffening fingers, he signed his name.

After the war, the young soldier in ragged uniform sought out the prominent judge. The servants refused to admit him because he looked like the many other tramps coming by for handouts.

He made a ruckus and insisted he see the judge. Finally, hearing the commotion, the judge came out and read the note. He at first was convinced it was another beggar's appeal. But he studied the signature, and even in its scribbled state he recognized it as his own son's.

He embraced the soldier, led him into his home, and said, with tears coursing down his cheeks, "You can have anything that my money can buy, and everything that my influence can secure."

What brought about the sudden change in the judge's attitude? It was the signature of his son, Charlie, affixed to the bottom of that note. It was the father-son relationship that made the difference.

There is an old saying in our world: "It's not *what* you know, it's *who* you know, that counts!"

That same principle holds true in the spiritual realm. All the knowledge in the world will not help you as you approach your Heavenly Father, but your personal relationship with Jesus Christ, the Son, will open to you all kinds of possibilities! It's not too late to make right that relationship with the Son, who will in turn provide you an access to the throne room of heaven!

Today's Quote: *All God's giants have been weak men who did great things for God because they reckoned on His being with them!* — J. Hudson Taylor

Today's Verse: "In that day you will no longer ask me anything. I tell you the truth, my Father will give you whatever you ask in my name" (John 16:23).

Day 26
The Failure

For more than 20 years, Robert Frost was a failure. He was considered a failure by friends, neighbors, and publishers. It was a lonely, frustrating struggle for recognition and publication, which never seemed willing to come his way. He often said that during this time he was one of the few persons who knew he was a poet.

The world has since mourned the passing of Robert Frost, and today he towers as one of America's greatest writers of verse. His poems have been published in 22 different languages at last count. The American edition of his poems has sold more than a million copies.

Frost was a four-time winner of the coveted Pulitzer Prize for poetry and had more honorary degrees thrust on him than any other man of letters. He was in constant demand to read his writings.

Robert Frost was 39 years old before he was able to sell his first volume of poetry to any publisher. For more than 20 long years, his writing was received by an endless stream of rejection slips, yet he kept on composing poems and submitting his work. Finally his perseverance paid off. He was published and considered a poet. Today we can say that the world is wiser and richer for the writings of Robert Frost.

An eminent psychiatrist, Dr. George Crane, recently listed various ingredients necessary for greatness. Among those qualities he noted are some you'd expect to find — talent, responsibility, etc.

Then, surprisingly, he said that physical stamina is also necessary! He reasons that many men do not reach the apex of their life endeavors until quite late in life and, therefore, endurance is necessary. He cited Winston Churchill as a prime example.

What is true in the physical realm of life is also true in the spiritual part of living. If we are to reach the ultimate in what God wants us to be, there must be spiritual endurance. This quality is called "long-suffering" as well as "patience" in the Bible. The apostle Paul even lists long-suffering as a fruit of the Spirit. In this journey on earth, it's the little things that drive us to despair. To reach your goal in life will take endurance. In the end, you'll be glad you didn't give up.

Today's Quote: *The battle against evil is difficult, not so much because of the action required, but because of the endurance necessary to achieve victory!* — Eleanor L. Doan

Today's Verse: But he that shall endure unto the end, the same shall be saved (Mark 13:13;KJV).

One father is worth more than a hundred schoolmasters.

George Herbert (1593–1633)

A Sympathetic Ear

A soldier in the Union army during the Civil War was a youngest son who had already lost his older brother and father in the terrible fighting. As the only male left in his family, he desired to go Washington, DC, to see President Lincoln and ask for an exemption from military service. His mother and sister needed him to help with the spring planting on the farm.

After receiving a leave from the military in order to plead his cause, he made his way to the White House. The young man approached the doors and asked to see the president.

He was told by the guard on duty, "You can't see the president. Don't you know there's a war on? The president's a very busy man. Now go away, Son! Get back out there and fight the Rebels!"

So the young man left, discouraged and downhearted. He stopped to sit on a park bench and a little boy came up to him. The young lad said, "Soldier, you look unhappy. What's wrong?"

The soldier looked at this young boy and began to spill his heart about his situation and how his father and older brother had died in the war. He explained that as the only male left in the family, he was desperately needed back at the farm for spring planting. The child listened to his entire story.

Then the little boy took the soldier by the hand and led him around to the back of the White House. They went through the kitchen door, past the guards on duty, past all the generals and high ranking government officials who were in the White House. All of these officials stood at attention as this little boy took the private by the hand through the rooms of the White House. The young soldier didn't understand all that was happening.

Finally, they arrived at the presidential office itself, and the little boy didn't even bother to knock; he just opened the door and walked in. There was President Lincoln with his secretary of state, looking over a map of battle plans on his desk.

The president looked up and said, "What can I do for you, Todd?"

And Todd said, "Daddy, this soldier needs to talk to you." The soldier pleaded his cause and received his exemption.

We, too, have access to the Father through the Son. Jesus intervenes on our behalf with, "Daddy, here is someone who needs to talk to You!"

Today's Quote: *What cannot be told to human ears can be poured into God's sympathetic ear!* — Eleanor Doan

Today's Verse: This then, is how you should pray: "Our Father in heaven, hallowed be your name" (Matt. 6:9).

The Scarred Stranger

A small orphaned boy lived with his grandmother. One night their house caught on fire, and the grandmother, attempting to rescue the boy who was asleep upstairs, perished in the flames. A crowd gathered around the burning house, and the boy's cries for help were heard above the crackling of the blaze. No one seemed to know what to do, for by this time the front of the house was a mass of flames.

Suddenly a stranger rushed from the crowd and circled to the back where he spotted an iron pipe that reached upstairs. He disappeared for a minute and then reappeared with the boy in his arms. Amid cheers, he climbed down the hot pipe as the boy hung around his neck.

Weeks later, a public hearing was held in the town hall to determine in whose custody the boy would be placed. Each person wanting the boy was allowed to speak briefly.

The first man said, "We have a big farm. Everybody needs the out-of-doors."

The second man told of the advantages he and his wife could provide. "I'm a teacher. I have a large library, and he would have an excellent education."

Others spoke, then finally the richest man in the small community said, "I am wealthy. I could give the boy everything already mentioned tonight — farm, education, and more, including money and travel. I'd like to take him home."

The judge asked, "Would anyone else like to say a word?"

From the back seat rose a stranger who had slipped into the hearing unnoticed. As he walked toward the front, deep suffering showed in his face. Reaching the front of the room, he stood directly in front of the little boy who sat with his head down. Slowly the stranger removed his hands from his pockets. A gasp went up from the crowd. The little boy — whose eyes had been focused on the floor until now — looked up. The man's hands were terribly scarred.

Suddenly the boy let out a cry of recognition. Here was the man who had saved his life. His hands were scarred from climbing up and down the hot pipe. With a leap of joy, he threw himself around the stranger's neck and held on for dear life.

The farmer rose to leave, the teacher, too, and then the richest man also left. Everyone else had also departed, leaving the boy and his rescuer to face the judge alone. The scarred stranger had won without a word!

Today's Quote: *Self-preservation is the first law of nature; self-sacrifice is the highest rule of grace!* — Unknown

Today's Verse: It is impossible for the blood of bulls and goats to take away sins (Heb. 10:4).

Day 29
Say Goodbye

An old man on the isle of Crete had loved many things during his lifetime. He loved his wife, his children, and his job, but most of all he loved the land. He loved the very ground he walked on, worked, and fought for. When it was time for him to die, he had his sons bring him outside his stone cottage and lay him on the hard earth. He reached down, grabbed a handful of Crete's soil and was gone.

He arrived at the gates of heaven, and the Lord came out dressed in the long robes of a judge and said to him, "Old man, come in."

As the old man moved toward the gates, the Lord noticed something in his hand and said, "What are you clutching in your hand?"

He said, "It is Crete. I go nowhere without it."

The Lord said, "Leave it, or you will not be allowed in."

The old man held his clenched fist up and said, "Never!" And he went and sat beside the outside wall of the heavenly city.

After a week had passed, the gates opened again. This time the Lord appeared in the guise of a man wearing a hat and looking like one of the old man's companions from Crete. He sat down next to the man and, putting His arm around his shoulder, said, "My friend, dust belongs in the wind. Drop that piece of earth and come inside."

But the old man was still adamant. He said, "Never!"

During the third week, the old man looked down at the earth he was clutching and saw that it had begun to cake and crumble. All of the moisture of the earth had gone out of it. Also, his fingers were arthritic and could not hold onto the dirt. The earth began to trickle through his fingers.

Once again the Lord appeared, this time as a small child. He came up to the old man, sat next to him, and said, "Grandfather, the gates only open for those with open hands."

The old man thought about this and finally stood up. He did not even look down as his hand opened and the crumbled dirt of Crete fell through the sky. The child took the man's hand and led him toward the glorious gates. As the gates swung open, he walked inside to find that heaven was all of Crete.

This story illustrates a point that many of us must be reminded of now and then. There is nothing here worth missing heaven in order to keep.

Today's Quote: *Many people hope to be elected to heaven who are not even running for the office!* — Author unknown

Today's Verse: And God shall wipe away all tears from their eyes; and there shall be no more death, neither sorrow, nor crying, neither shall there be any more pain: for the former things are passed away (Rev. 21:4;KJV).

Day 30
Are You?

Shortly after World War II came to a close, Europe began to pick up the pieces. Much of the continent had been ravaged by war and was in ruins. The saddest sight of all, however, was that of little orphaned children starving and roaming the streets of those war-torn cities.

Early one chilly morning, an American soldier was making his way back to the barracks in London. As he turned a corner with his jeep he spotted a little boy dressed in tattered clothes, standing with his nose pressed against the window of a bakery. Inside, the baker was kneading dough for a fresh batch of donuts. The hungry boy stared in silence, watching every move of the baker.

The soldier pulled his jeep to the curb, got out, and walked quietly over to where the little guy stood. He did this unnoticed by the child.

Through the steamed-up window, the orphan could see the mouthwatering morsels as they were being dipped out of the huge skillet in which they were being made. They were piping hot. The boy watched as the donuts were covered with powered sugar and others were glazed with frosting. Salivating with hunger, the child let out a slight groan as he watched the baker carefully place them into the glass enclosed counter for sale.

The soldier's heart went out to the little one who stood beside him. "Son, would you like some of those?" the soldier broke into the silence.

Startled, the boy looked up at the soldier and with enthusiasm, said, "Oh, yes! I would!"

The American GI stepped inside and bought a dozen of those delicious donuts. Then, taking the sack from the baker, walked outside to where the lad was standing in the cold, foggy London morning. He smiled, held out the bag, and simply said, "Here you are."

As the soldier turned to walk back to his jeep, he felt an insistent tug on his coat. He stopped, turned around and looked at the little boy. The child asked quietly, "Mister, are you God?"

We are never more like God than when we give, when we are touched with compassion, and when we act on that compassion. The Bible, in it's most familiar verse says, "God so loved the world that He gave. . . ." All of us have something to give to someone, today.

Today's Quote: *You can't help another person uphill without getting closer to the top yourself!* — Unknown

Today's Verse: Then Peter said, "Silver or gold I do not have, but what I have I give you. In the name of Jesus Christ of Nazareth, walk" (Acts 3:6).